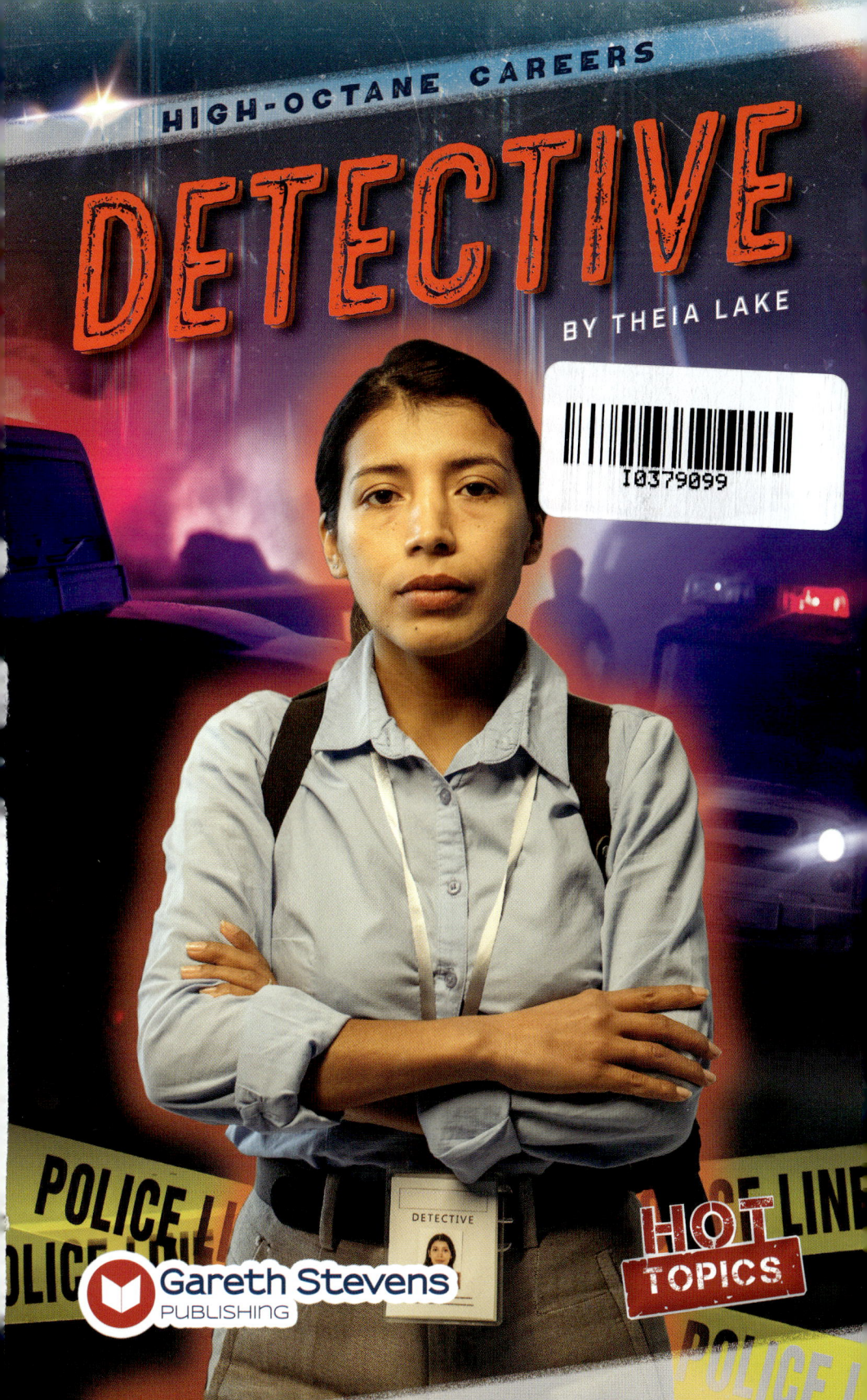

Please visit our website, www.garethstevens.com. For a free color catalog of all our high-quality books, call toll free 1-800-542-2595 or fax 1-877-542-2596.

Cataloging-in-Publication Data

Names: Lake, Theia.
Title: Detective / Theia Lake.
Description: Buffalo, NY : Gareth Stevens Publishing, 2025. | Series: High-octane careers | Includes glossary.
Identifiers: ISBN 9781482469202 (pbk.) | ISBN 9781482469219 (library bound) | ISBN 9781482469226 (ebook)
Subjects: LCSH: Detectives–Juvenile literature. | Criminal justice administration–Juvenile literature.
Classification: LCC HV7922.L25 2025 | DDC 363.2–dc23

Published in 2025 by
Gareth Stevens Publishing
2544 Clinton Street
Buffalo, NY 14224

Copyright © 2025 Gareth Stevens Publishing

Designer: Claire Zimmermann
Editor: Theresa Emminizer

Photo credits: Cover, p. 1 (woman) Pressmaster/Shutterstock.com; cover, p.1 (emergency lights background) zef art/Shutterstock.com; cover, pp. 1, 7 (police tape) Gorodenkoff/Shutterstock.com; cover, p.1 (series title light flare) SpicyTruffel/Shutterstock.com; series art (background texture) Golubovy/Shutterstock.com; series art (page number scribble) ozzichka /Shutterstock.com; pp. 5, 25 SeventyFour/Shutterstock.com; pp. 7, 15 Gorodenkoff/Shutterstock.com; pp. 9, 27 Krakenimages.com/Shutterstock.com; p. 11 felipe caparros/Shutterstock.com; p. 13 DC Studio/Shutterstock.com; p. 17 Standret/Shutterstock.com; p. 19 Drazen Zigic/Shutterstock.com; p. 21 VGstockstudio/Shutterstock.com; p. 23 a katz/Shutterstock.com; p. 29 BearFotos/Shutterstock.com; p. 30 (icons) smx12/Shutterstock.com, (camera and microscope icons) Trimaker/Shutterstock.com.

Some of the images in this book illustrate individuals who are models. The depictions do not imply actual situations or events.

All rights reserved. No part of this book may be reproduced in any form without permission in writing from the publisher, except by a reviewer.

Printed in the United States of America

CPSIA compliance information: Batch #CWGS25: For further information contact Gareth Stevens, at 1-800-542-2595.

Find us on

CONTENTS

Crime Solvers 4
At the Scene 6
Conducting Interviews 8
Analyzing Evidence 10
Building a Case 12
In the Courtroom 14
Types of Detectives 16
Education 18
Experience 20
Special Training 22
Sleuth Skills 24
On the Job 26
Get Started! 28
Criminal Justice Careers 30
For More Information 31
Glossary 32
Index 32

CRIME SOLVERS

Do you enjoy mystery stories? Do you get excited about looking for clues and hunting for answers? If so, you might want to be a detective! Detectives **solve** crimes. They gather evidence, or facts, to uncover the truth about what happened.

UNDER PRESSURE!

When a crime happens, detectives are part of the investigation. An investigation is when all the facts about a crime are studied closely and carefully.

AT THE SCENE

The first step of an investigation is to visit the crime scene. Detectives work closely with police and other crime scene specialists. Specialists take pictures and carefully collect evidence. Detectives walk through the scene, taking note of everything they see.

UNDER PRESSURE!

At the scene, police officers and detectives may find witnesses and ask them questions about what happened. Witnesses are people who see a crime.

CONDUCTING INTERVIEWS

Detectives talk to witnesses to piece together what happened during the crime. They also interview, or talk to, possible suspects. A suspect is someone who may have committed, or done, a crime. Studying evidence helps detectives identify, or figure out, who is a possible suspect.

UNDER PRESSURE!

Detectives also speak to victims. A victim is a person who a crime was committed against. Sometimes victims can identify who committed a crime, sometimes they can't.

ANALYZING EVIDENCE

Forensic specialists analyze, or study, evidence such as fingerprints, footprints, handwriting, and DNA found at the scene. They share their findings with detectives, who use this information to identify suspects. Detectives may also investigate **digital** evidence, such as computer or phone records.

UNDER PRESSURE!

DNA is the part of the body that carries genetic information. Everyone's DNA is unique, or one-of-a-kind. DNA evidence includes hair, blood, and saliva, or spit!

BUILDING A CASE

Detectives keep **detailed** records of the evidence, interviews, and information they gather. There are many laws and rules about how evidence should be collected and preserved, or kept. If these rules aren't followed, the evidence may be dismissed, or thrown out, in court.

UNDER PRESSURE!

Detectives put all the facts about a case into a report. This report must be clear and organized. It will be used to build a case.

IN THE COURTROOM

Detectives are often called on to testify, or speak, in court. They talk about the findings of their investigation, giving more information about the evidence that's been presented, and stating their **professional** ideas about what happened. The detective's testimony is a key part of prosecuting criminals.

UNDER PRESSURE!

Prosecution is bringing legal action against someone. A detective's testimony can be used to support, or back, the case of the prosecution.

TYPES OF DETECTIVES

There are different kinds of detectives.

- Homicide detectives investigate murders (killings) and deaths.
- Fraud detectives investigate criminal deception (lies).
- Cybercrime detectives investigate internet crimes.
- Narcotics detectives investigate drug crimes.
- Missing persons detectives find missing people.
- Cold case detectives investigate unsolved cases.

EDUCATION

Detectives need at least a high school education. However, it's helpful to go on to earn an associate's (two year) **degree** or bachelor's (four year) degree in a related field. Related fields include criminal justice, criminology, and forensic science.

UNDER PRESSURE!

The requirements, or things that are needed, to become a detective are different depending on what kind of detective you want to be and where you want to work.

EXPERIENCE

To become a detective, you need **experience** in law enforcement, or police work. Many detectives start out as police officers. That means meeting police requirements and training at a police academy, or school. Law enforcement experience helps detectives better understand crimes that may happen.

UNDER PRESSURE!

To work in law enforcement, you must be 21 years old, have a driver's license, and have a clean criminal record. You must also pass special tests.

SPECIAL TRAINING

Once a person has earned the required education and experience for their academy and jurisdiction (area of practice), they can **apply** to become a detective. Detectives usually need to go through a training program to learn more specialized skills and techniques, or ways of doing things.

UNDER PRESSURE!

Police officers and detectives must be able to pass fitness (strength), hearing, and vision (sight) tests. They must also pass drug tests.

SLEUTH SKILLS

Detective work is a high-**stress** job. Detectives need strong minds to deal with crimes. They also need to be deep thinkers, good problem-solvers, and strong leaders. To get the answers they need, detectives must communicate well with witnesses, victims, suspects, and teammates.

ON THE JOB

Since they work on crime scenes, detectives often see very bad things. They spend time in unsafe places and have to deal with dangerous criminals. Detectives often work long hours at all times of the day and night while investigating a case.

UNDER PRESSURE!

Although detectives are trained to deal with scary crimes, it's very important for them to continue to take care of their health and well-being.

GET STARTED!

Does being a detective sound exciting to you? Strengthen your sleuthing skills by reading mystery books! Visit an **escape room** or throw a murder mystery party! Do puzzles, play games, and find more fun ways to get started today.

CRIMINAL JUSTICE CAREERS

How a detective's salary compare to other criminal justice jobs? Take a look at this chart to find out!

MEDIAN SALARIES IN CRIMINAL JUSTICE

Crime Scene Investigator	$47,800
Forensic Photographer	$49,300
Private Investigator	$50,510
Forensic Science Technician	$59,150
Police Officer	$65,170
Computer & Digital Forensic Analyst	$73,900
Detective	$83,170
Judge	$97,870
Lawyer	$122,960

INDEX

criminal justice,
18
criminology, 18
DNA, 10, 11
evidence, 4, 6, 8,
10, 11, 12, 14
forensic science,
18

investigate, 5, 6,
16, 26
law
enforcement,
20, 21
mystery, 4, 28
prosecution, 15
report, 13

suspect, 8, 10,
24
testify, 14, 15
victim, 9, 24
witness, 7, 24

GLOSSARY

apply: To officially ask for something.

degree: An official paper given to someone who has completed certain classes at a college or university.

detailed: Having lots of small parts.

digital: Having to do with computer technology.

escape room: A room people are locked in so they can play a game requiring them to solve a series of puzzles within a certain amount of time to accomplish a goal.

forensic: Having to do with applying science to solve a problem or answer a question.

experience: Skills gained by doing something.

professional: Having to do with a job.

solve: To find the answer.

stress: A state of concern, worry, or feeling nervous.

FOR MORE INFORMATION

BOOKS

Morkes, Andrew. *Police Officer and Detective.* Philadelphia, PA: Mason Crest, 2022.

Rowan, Jennifer. *Crime Scene: Collecting Physical Evidence.* Hollywood, FL: Mason Crest Publishers, 2022.

WEBSITES

50 States
www.50states.com/education/careers/criminal-justice-careers/

Learn more about careers in criminal justice.

Little Explainers
www.littleexplainers.com/how-to-explain-evidence-to-a-child/#The_Role_of_a_Detective

Find out how detectives collect and analyze evidence and try your own experiments!

Publisher's note to educators and parents: Our editors have carefully reviewed these websites to ensure that they are suitable for students. Many websites change frequently, however, and we cannot guarantee that a site's future contents will continue to meet our high standards of quality and educational value. Be advised that students should be closely supervised whenever they access the internet.